DATE DUE

NOV 25 2003		
JUN 0 4 2005		

Other books by Dennis Phillips

The Hero Is Nothing (1985)
A World (1989)
Arena (1991)
Means (1991)
20 Questions (1992)
Book of Hours (1996)
Credence (1996)
Study for the Ideal City (1999)

SAND

Dennis Phillips

GREEN INTEGER
KØBENHAVN & LOS ANGELES
2002

GREEN INTEGER BOOKS
Edited by Per Bregne
København/Los Angeles

Distributed in the United States by Consortium Book
Sales and Distribution, 1045 Westgate Drive, Suite 90
Saint Paul, Minnesota 55114–1065

(323) 857-1115/http://www.greeninteger.com

First Edition 2002
©2002 by Dennis Phillips
Portions of this book were previously published in
Angles, Disturbed Guillotine, Lyric &, New American Writing,
Rhizome, Ribot, Untitled, and *Volt.*
Back cover copy ©2002 by Green Integer

Design: Per Bregne
Typography: Barbara Maloutas
Cover: Photograph of Dennis Phillips by
Courtney Gregg

LIBRARY OF CONGRESS CATALOGING IN PUBLICATION DATA
Dennis Phillips [1951]
Sand
ISBN: 1-931243-43-3
p. cm — Green Integer 67
I. Title II. Series

Green Integer books are published for Douglas Messerli
Printed in the United States of America on acid-free paper.

for Courtney

1 Prelude

They once said clear but now the comma's indistinct.

To seek one's purchase, they said.
Or they too may imitate.

They may sit together in a selected group.
Explosions are expected,
the sky is clear and a fragrance hovers unacknowledged.

Even then they saw the meaning entrenched.

2 Altered Landscape

These are the quotes, they said.

These symbols are accomplishments.

Troops, someone said.

The effect is too general. These
correspondences, just gilded,
tremendous in emptiness.

Repose is the compliment of which value?
Distance? Relation? Volume?

We were there, we saw them.
These are their responses, as if
witnessing or cavalry
attended these factors.

It hadn't seemed abnormal to alter the landscape with a mound of excavated dirt.

Economics and ecology: the parts they chose, they being others, not earlier referents, the plants existing far away and separate from altered terrain.

Or the fishing fleet (three boats) for example. They separate still. We call them less opera than wind chop, less opinion than the delusion of habit lets us call an ocean a prairie.

In a specially prepared history it had not seemed abnormal to leave out the parts which might distract others from the point thought most important.

The ships so radical their captains without compass. The crews keep waiting for the music to start or the voice-over.

Somewhere time is measured by pages. Strata would also work.

The plants once kept far away now have tours. Did you think we meant country matters? Or by compass did you mean terrain?

They undercut the ridge upland
or clouds pour down slope

Here is a challenge:
You take green and I'll take red

Or here is a challenge:
Demonstrate or they doubt you

A submerged plain,
they open a tool box: only a tempo

A common vista we surrender

As emptiness seems to preside. Their faces were upturned, eyes carefully covered, as they must have known. Yes, a herd of bison, this early, the cave record, yes, a frail romance. Having opened the topic a crying or whining or squeaking was heard. Were they aware of the error? She or he remembered the face but not its name. The shift of possibilities quickly flipping through his or her mental catalogue. The phone had rung only a dozen times. Not even the chance of injury was possible. Autumn seemed near or was that a speech rehearsed?

Light beaded at the structure's chines
as a language spoken by a few thousand people.
A cold level rests under.
Expect a tide every half-life.

Reliant on observation, dependent on promptitude.
Excited by the tardy, enthralled by the oblivious.

The only response unrehearsed
would be the particulars of flora and fauna
or a record kept of habits, depths and phases.

They had found that inevitabilities were not always agreeable. Their behaviors and thus their pleasures diminished. Nothing as it perfectly could be.

Overtly a comma is insinuated but we can't say from where. Their desire is to weaken us with our own terms: the idea of being literal or the precarious trait of projecting into a deduced future.

They had stumbled. The road was unfinished. The signs had warned them. In the other room, on a tv, a voice projected sadness.

So this time they wandered, crossed a border then a threshold or that's what they believed.

No turning point but the business trips were deadly.

Earlier the simple puzzle was too taxing.

And so reports from only one field. And yet nothing would stay with him: the nine line form he invented, bronze, her position apart. He was dealing with obsessions. The face on the face of the head he remembered. A phone call, dozens of phone calls.

Further away an island.

The impatient abecedarian. Every letter every correspon-
dent sound every numerical equivalent every suggested
construct every actual image every idea.

Finally weather moved across the basin with humid air the preface, thunder and lightning the footnotes.

It had been late. They started with a title and a specific length. Carrying forward it was easy to get started. But the concept of carrying forward was too abstract. The voice was the receiver. They had asked for cliffs and sea shore but had run out of patience. They had thought to suspend him above the audience but finally a platform would suffice. They knew that standing still had never been his problem.

It was definitely the mathematical reality of running out. Or so they postured.

Their only horizon an air pocket.

Rather than concourse, a paving stone.

Although they had commissioned the portrait, no one had organized the proper way of responding.

These images could be considered recurrent, appearing at least once a year. The tone is alarming, the light's color and timbre consistent. They heard of a rumor or echo which reminded them of the human voice, a report some called it.

They mistook time for line.

They encouraged their visitors toward stealth.

Reading the biographies of persons in Paris may have put their guests in jeopardy.

An arrangement could be made to meet others. And yet now a cloud could clearly be seen.

If the light were disagreeable then who would have the right to complain? Acknowledging an editorial habit, we were pure. Panic can be suppressed. We saw the report. Costly thy habit. The presence of the human voice. Some we can't see. Poles or antipodes as fellows dwell.

Though several of them thought her too literal, she claimed the ability of extracting silver and gold from sunlight.

3 Hidden Proof

But then nothing was
surprising or at least on schedule.

Imagine the distrustful looking down
in a volcanic setting or at any of the high points.

The noise of a village, a wind shift.

Or it's the details in the postcards they send: The fog bank, which is to say airiness; the references expunged from the walls; their hidden proofs older than argument. In the photo we appear to be listening: There is silver in their ink stains.

Clear, pine trees and asphalt, dry, a smell was coming and I went east, and up, but the compass confirmed it, woodpeckers also near, a comfort to those who misread. The idea of "It seems as if it were yesterday" really means clarity, a town nearby, wind too similar to cars approaching, upwelling bound to occur, waiting for the truck to come, there they are, a family, any family: their house

Because there is no context
there's a point of contact
in a dark room.
Important people are spot lit.
Emphasis on ties.

In the shade of a comment
a boreal wind chill
a curve never noticed before
light blocked
that once flowed freely
a spectrum broken
that once had seemed a bridge.

4 Island Thinking

Only to realize that there was no one else.

Yet each mutation no matter how small,
adds traces of induplicatability.

The rock is so porous it floats,
no matter what had been previously dissolved.

Having the landscape or not knowing it.

On one's own, time flattened really, obverse:
object, subject, dawn or dusk. No coordinates.

Accordingly, a missile, the way they call any thrown thing a missile. The reference to sleep an accident. I.e. what is the sleeper to the person in the dream?

Withdrawing to a safer post, they quickly noticed an activity. Each fraction of a degree of temperature was felt in dramatic, sometimes convulsive ways.

The vessel, the shadow of the vessel, the shadow alone.

Compulsive is the family that has no heat.

This is the moment. Their urgent fucking daisy chain, i.e. the future, i.e. when he returned the news was even.

To see grey and call it blue. Or cornered by any convention and by that we mean trapped, a figure of speech, thus artifice.

But they were given a general field of choices, temperate weather among them, absent of event, burgeoning with landscape.

Do not read this as if the mirror were a serious concern. It is not liquid.

When the stirring in the loins
where some scale could be enforced
incessant coupling
omnidirectional.
Thanatos.

My over silence.

Crept between sheets.
The small tiles they complain of.

This is island thinking.

The whisper, not an appropriate ending.
The hotel's adrift, placeless, postless
as if a logical argument
or the world of judgment.

Proportioned without accent
these are disagreements
the humidity a new topic
bird song, wind drone, water drying
a quarter beyond silent
a blended weather, a knotted,
whether withheld offerings
or a wind–borne, avian winter.

5 Fields Surrounded

How loose they become they said.
His story close to history.
Sanctum. Or hear it their way.

They might raise questions and yet variable lines are pursued as anyone might imagine.

Thus the strategy was confirmed
 just as those around the table felt it had lost its meaning.

When quizzed later, no one remembered
that the tasks assigned resembled a form they had sought,
almost automatically, to avoid.

Sanctorum. Or withholding a formed idea.

Though the alternate came closer.

Walking into the rain forest.

As plans congealed she noticed her attitude.
This is the plane advance on oblique problems.
Being thus exposed, feeling naked without a continental
    shelf,
and yet things arranged and contacts made.

A hiatus would make little difference.

You have been consistently surprised by the retention of
    others.
And yet retentiveness is its own problem.

In the water despite your fear of combining solids and
    fluids
despite a humming you can hear in silence,

or in the seat of power, making a study of randomness,
desirous of prediction, they will always see us as
interlopers.

Rather than record them
rather than acknowledge a "through line"
beginning to make a market.
Or further away,
if fogless
then nearer,
a journey
as far as the rocks.

In the shade of a stiff wind. A smoothing over, i.e., polymers, grass fields. The urges or demiurges. The lens cap is missing or will be missing. A narrow Umbrian way, and by relaxing, stone, wood. The view of a rumor of a view. Sound in a medium without adhesion. Report of a sighting.

By waiting or did they say wishing.

Numerous though they were.

The apparent abuse the sisters endured
at the mercy of their dates.

It became still, windless, eerie.

What if what they said had happened?

Gradually one is surrounded by ghosts.

Surrounded by increments (geologically speaking)
as if the very nature of self-consciousness
were strata which seem
consumptive of time,
the list you make, the catalogue.

And so she was rueful
and yet showed up.

Take for example the process of temple building
tempered and layered in artifact
from rock to powder to fluid.

6 Formal Cornerings

There is rain at the horizon
a chill but the moon, gibbous,
is out of sight the tides severe
and automatic. Or turn
to remove this.

You will ask about decay
and the rest of the auditors
will congratulate a certain spirit
they can't help but misquote.
In fervent belief.

The sharks will rest now
but some believe that sharks once growled like wolves
and consumed elephants
caught in a renegade tide.

Mournfully, but that starts us toward prejudice. Possibly everything soaks up quickly, without trace. It may be the military, the featureless flats, the easy silhouettes, or researchers perhaps.

Though some say things (events) happen in sets of three others say that an event (thing) far away removes pressure from other things (events) about to occur nearby.

On the occasion of slow-moving cells, from the northwest, which happen without musical assistance, darker than the back of a house,

a shadow, flat on rippled steel, and if that's not poetic enough, a sound, flat in waves of rain, the coastal the up-slope wind, whispers a mile away.

As if air could gather.

The stealth of, not silence but flatness. Yet some things *are* mournful. Humidity too, a sudden voice out of sleep.

Slow-moving researchers, cells too passive, a silver sleep, a silver wind, a silver watch, a camera.

To find the time he thought it was darker by the room to the right an archive of rooms although clocks of all types and measures and dividers the sudden quiet imposed by utility can attract as well as repel or that darkness is one part of a concept which married to its opposite creates a state into which our minds cannot wander i.e. the absence of both light and dark or the landscape it might conjure something terminal some distance called a waste a term whose history is not equal to the condition it seeks to describe so flimsy so filmy here, heaven, locked.

This explained their curious detachment. Of the several possibilities opened, only the most remote form erupted. The calm vistas were false idols. Any entanglement bore the serious chance of misunderstanding. So history and philosophy and psychology were overcoats that might or might not be appropriate in fit or function. Who said who? The fabric is that fragile. Yes, in the tranquilized hours. Beginners in the sands of an outgrown clod.

Finally a settling occurs and your footsteps set in finally, in precise detail and a rhythm is offered and we are amazed at the darkness the silence the list of accounted things.

As earnestly as they had hankered a hunger a lust earnestly recovered mountainously.

Knowing it was always in the wings so to speak, wings being a theatrical reference which sounds avian, as opposed to waiting, a temporal reference which sounds like volume.

This was freedom. Because confinement was so productive?

Thus the phone calls became essential. Each word they spoke reverberated through the room's black shades (red to them) a political matrix, outlined and so arousing that they too had to act (the shades or the callers?).

Others say that the sun had grown too hot. Nothing could stay solid. Still others, that a county away the climate steadily improved.

Who were they to question their resources?

As if a simple implantation, fantasy or truth-telling, a feast day, the way a new idea (technology) will always seem threatening, one smiles, the end is sightlessly measured but linearly.

And so they who would like to give it or they who withhold it or they are characters and may do anything.

Subtract something but even that is history, or graft something on, their journeys to distant capitals, for example: they who reign so popular.

7 The Lost Nickel

The sound of the gate at an hour when the gate sounds.

One list covers the subject.

Is the returning of messages a diminutive of Return Fantasy?

The role of the electron is different on paper.

The sound of a warning horn when the *all clear* is sounded.

The lost nickel. You define your universe.
Sanguine, the way paper bleeds through.

The return, i.e. even after seconds
the thought was not retained.

A narcotic will be applied or ingested.

And then colors, emerging as if the skin were too weak.

Your parallel harmonies, even the words are subsumed.

This is the coin of your crossing.

Murmurs or echoes or animals; you will not suggest a
    gender.

This is not the fulfilling of a program.

The voices carry, you see.

It was only the bamboo, a form of grass.

His initial reaction was to imagine himself borne down, not under the surface of fluid but into a vacuum that was only what he was before birth.

To them the problem was presenting what they knew.

But why should the temporary be difficult to understand?

The lost nickel.

Deflection i.e. someone else's attempt to steer the universe, or admit to what?

Now the winds come up which are almost the same as earthquakes.

Is it the plain knowledge of an unencumbered self analyst or the blind residue of an age too attached to something it calls certain?

Taken as a single event the earth
at least give it credit for its prose,
the shifts, if properly punctuated
here's the result of always quantifying,
that is, the phone remains silent,
Ahab's magnetic ascendance is measured.

Taken as a single event the earth
or take the fauna just as an example
the verdant hour, escapades voiced
there's no such distance harmonically
or atonally the tones coalescent
that is, external, fretless but alarming
the windows rattle, the birds stop.

Taken as a pattern, emergent, interrupted
or so rests our sciences, as if to really believe something,
form, for example, is to tie to biology,
as a single event, in the era and the world of inducement.

Taken as an illusion then, would that work
or do our bowels loosen too much in the low frequency
when it's high frequency we crave
steel against steel at a certain Fahrenheit
or something with a continuity other than time?

Taken as an allotment of no discernable amount,
of no discernable length.

8 Attention to Details

As if a preceding power had transformed them to horses.

Their attention turned again in details. No matter how often the issue of distance was raised it was rarely grasped. The hall they gather in fills with their own humidity. Proximity to the city is noticed by thickening.

Their inattention is sometimes diverted as people around them speak to themselves. A small place was planned for and this was irrelevant. The letters they remember seem so compelling. Or any of the tokens of their pasts. Don't you see, the effect is far more complex than simple self-absorption. They think about the mental map they automatically form which places sentences in a landscape they can never convey.

An act of abandonment can be defined variously and subjectively. This is not a theory. The body is a burden of enormous pleasure. The burden might be its brevity. The mark we made in the wedge of light by the doorway at night at the top of the stairs, in a city we can't remember during a year we must have spent.

Their ordered perceptions.
I.e. the retail of finality.
The poor formality, the overtly finite.

A culmination of rituals.
The visitor is sleek but evasive.
A residue, a record of commitments,
a claim hyperbolic.

Voices are always at the door.
This happens automatically.

They see the red light in their pupils.
The commentators will not stop their commentary.
The senators will not hold.
Their retinas blaze in a literal code.

Don't cry at the sound of breathing
a centerboard would be sufficient.

A cover will be an overstatement
no matter how tight the mesh.
The safety of the match is not our concern.

A squabble between them.

This is the constitution of our deception,
a confluence of covers.

It is so sweet, they said, so calm, so peaceful.
It was, he said, the most profound sound he'd ever heard.

•

Now, above you all, and by that the author means himself
(known) and the reader (unknown), above you all are the
simplified icons of an occupation, which could refer to
military or economic domination or a job, but curiously
not to thought, although preoccupation suggests a state of
thinking but not a condition preliminary to domination
except insofar as thought or its analogue precedes most
complex actions. Letters, which might be missives or parts
of an alphabet, will not arrive in time to stop a chain of
events a great distance away, where strategy and informa-

tion are crucial. There is a tonality of catastrophe, accompanied, in the mind of the author, by specific mental maps that don't match the landscape or can't be conveyed, which could mean transported, translated or made translucent. The husk, hence, is all that can be offered.

•

On gelid
metal skin.

You may not proceed.
The methods of belief they supply you alternate.
The way is blocked.
Their request
in an age of confluence:
messageless

•

The sheets are clean. The oven announces us.

9 A World Littered with Vanishing Points

Suppose only one plan, they plead, but the streets are too steep. For example, it's the sides are too steep. But that's not what they meant by internal.

We cannot include among the tragedies those things which are simply forgotten.

Taken another way: It is always the same time of year when those who are considered strangers or observers arrive. This is the middle of the beginning of a puzzle that is always solved the same way.

Or was this a new city where nothing made sense and if it did, was the lack of sense intrinsic to the place or intrinsic to the visitor? The piazzas very empty and the shadows very long.

Yet even here – has a locale been suggested? – in the shadows are fractures. And though they mill around or find ways of expressing their needs, a cupola, invisible to them inside, is detailed and cold outside. High on the roof the moonlight's sufficient.

Here a corner induced
air ways so deceptive
a feminine voice here prolonged
an electric thing.

A complex music
the reeds dry
a post-mortem.

We picture an island of fragments
where the poet sweeps her floor
in pieces.

Many of the hostages
who are not always responsible
huddle behind curtains
deep in the rain forest.

This may or may not be your judgment.
A career hovers over the western sky
among the feelings of dismay.

What a job is the derivation of names.
An eclipse drove them crazy.
A cackling could be heard.

Though none of them divined location
which could also include time,
though some had noted a difference,
a decadence was more apparent,
leading us to another eclipse in the record.

Why did they sleep so insistently?

A reverence was performed.
Humbly we thank thee.
The price of traveling eastward.

The metal in the casements bowed.
Something in the labeling caused them to pause.

10 Forms of Promise

Smoothed
a scar.

•

Force a smooth thing

We come to be done

The politic easier
with fewer options
the world simple.

•

Smooth seamed
scarred a name
we can't recall
torpidly we convince ourselves
this their form of promise
a hatred thoroughly refused
skin popping through the bones
the first conferences
the carefully watched gestures
each headache
a formal nod.

A tempest would be the only revenge.

Our true cross identical to the other
and hence the trembling confession,
counted as shapes catalogued by rhythm.
Of course we believe it
or believe a portrait.

Breathe in, feed out.

This is science. How fortunate
the empirical.

You are waiting
in an aura of light
in a metal room
displacing more volume
than watching can compensate.

Nothing prefigures.
Accordingly we marry ideas to proofs

Their storm reports a clearing.
They would say to count the holes in the ceiling.
There are words for what normally we call things.

Though we could address these things at right angles
the peripheral is preferable.

Allusions to bombing could also be seen as personal.

A counter has rewards due
a counter is timely also.

Yet there resides a thought
deposited a thousand miles away
where no recipient listens.

Impulsivity is a narcotic
because once done nothing can be undone
noting the obvious, revising fate,
a counter's job in private.

The way a new presence takes a new space.
The primrose path of reason.

Out of which compression
which story?

Then any practice towards any mystery.

The idea of modes or location or place
stands how in the mere opposition of desires?

They knew before setting out that they might be
    disappointed.
Weathers, among the factors, were, of course, not
    predictable.

What they might change:
the terms they had become used to using
to describe themselves.

But going too far was problematic not only as a worry.

Why, for example, might one luxuriate in one rhythm
and agonize in another?

These are the memories they enfolded in an archive.
A chronicle that bemoans the loss of its perfection,
its modesty never tested.

When he returned his house had been emptied.
Neighbors said men had come.

Around the pool.
This would be summer.
At night concrete is warm.
Light from under water
the lantern, the pale cast upward
their faces still too distant to see.

This was her greatest claim against him,
as if a suggestion of place carries weight or creates an
    impact.
The impact of migrating mammals is easy to minimize
    but difficult to misunderstand.

Perspective is not necessarily the truth.

In some lips' taut vice
as the sun returns to our sky
and directions (cardinal) are restored.
In a tidal emergency inland is never far enough.

There is a way to say this.

In an intimate moment
when nothing but precision would hold.

The holding pattern, an aftertaste.

Their strict voices curtailed.

Their calm received in politeness.

Only the truly gifted will emerge from the stupor.

Shunting the vein often enough.

Coming up for air is not the same as air time.

Your presence is more than an eyeful.
Do they know what it means to be looked at?

Sitting and waiting: their aspiration for us.

There will always be a way to marry the interests of some
with their desire for more.

The calm received in politeness.

11 Tangle of Transparency

How can we formulate a wedge in the surface tension
if the sound is impossibly coded, he says
as in the old days
adrenaline seems to prevail
and species thought lost gather.
His window, his postmark.

This is the moment when even a promise can bead up,

When even the procession of scenarios must stop
and yet they don't stop. Altitude, perhaps, he considers,
light later and later now that he's fixed on it.

As unaware as he was of being a figure in someone's
    dream.

I pull the boat up the boat ramp.
On the beach no one believes the pressures.

Your holiday is quietly subverting you.
The equator is neutral in this act.

Grains of rice caulk the broken laminations.
We remember a time when the giant city was a shanty
    town.

I have spread out several bolts of cloth to dry.
You receive calls but may not return them.

All of the intricate chains of numbers I once knew,
all of the windows, the pearls, the magma I counted on.

There is a tangle and this is ancient.

No sorrow can be recorded.

The yellow tinge of the lawns has subsided.
The crude truth now.

Just finding the pins they used
becomes a lease on any clarity.

Their trains rendered transparent.

We cannot remember the commencement.
We cannot remember the highlights.
A sorrowful lake front,
clouds of suspicious velocity,
or other pictures
that still evoke the desire
for a whole story.

Or is this the depiction of a market ideal,
each day a palliative for the next?

Who walks the boundaries.   The sky is red.

And yet the hours freeze and stop calibrating.

Often the line is obscured, overgrown, shrouded.

A white hotel but it's only a trick of bear howl
and snow and desire.

We used to know something
but knowledge subsumes certainty.

A density without perspective.
A wild dog or wolf also freezes
but transparency evades us.

12 Shadows of Motive

Or that's where they keep their coils of rope and hose,
this island we remember, the exact temperature,
colored earth, the problem we can't regret.

There were messages and messages returned.
According to the cycles or regions or dogmas
the notion of place must be broadly applied.

They engineer so carefully to avoid repetition.
The voice we long for is never the same.

The cave or the description of the cave.
A gathering in the shadows of motive.

Whose voice or how numerous that phase becomes
here, emptied of starlight, flooded.

Whose voice, a pole apart from reason?
Because sense or any exiting wrinkles us,
eludes us.

These obstacles:
A courtly bow, the too resonant phrase, hope.

This misstep: A federal impulse,
whose voice we render necessarily false.

Mapped in quarters, redundant in images
a track, this track, exuberant without certainty.

Nor because every prediction's defeated.

This lecture they vaunted far from civilization
but, correct me, the lines are so melodic, the map's
only partly responsible for what they follow,
and the lecture, so slow and quaint, as if Africa
really could be summed up by half an hour of music.

So the expectation, tilled open, and those dreams
(we attach so many projections)
the sounds from the other rooms
the figures only visible peripherally
no matter from where they emerge.

The dry season was upon them the seepage
which defeated even concrete and steel
had only dissolved their ramparts
the cataracts now only visual,
the cliffs so quiet, so still.

Nor can every time be the same.

Things have happened although dreams can suggest a
    history.

The silence of expectation is worse.

What is it about paper that evokes the sensation of
    permanence?

A select group of people is carried along
for example how hills shockingly vivid
either do or do not find a place
and so those which remain remain forever.

The accumulation is astounding.

Carried along means remembered.
What temporary means is confusing still.

13 Committee Work

Nor thralled by magnitude (depth or horizon)
nor tumid in speed (sexual reference preferred)
but thralled and tumid on a hump of fluid
in the clear single lighting of an examined thing.

Because time is the factor they grant
we shall not simper before the kegs they possess
an indigo light fusing equal memories.

Had the answer been insufficient the corps might wither,
the multitude might weaken, the instructions' gravity
commands co-operation "if only we could bottle it."
Faces lit in the light of their exchange.

In this world the elect are pristine.

The soft face
under whose force she
revised as in yet another pronunciation.

Her story then.

The house was full. No calls nor deep
nor long employed without paper.
This is how they enforce their codicils.

Imply a tension.
Or a shade implied by umbrage taken.

It is raining on the peninsula and dark.

You said you lived there.

When the floods came even the routine was interrupted.

I remember crying, even for the memory of a melody
he told her.

Each promise or statement equals a temptation
and yet holding to a story can often create history.

You said they still were angry.
This was more about alignment.
They are the note-writers we never see.

The way sitting down is internal
or hoping for a nod
separates a desire for cunning
from the cobbling sound of stones
tumbled in waters shocked

It's too early now
in the landscape or town you picture
the very idea of sequence is something you can't compass.

The way they place you on a deck
and all the types of things they call decks.

"My God!" they are likely to have ejaculated or said.
Their gift suddenly sours.
We know that separate worlds remain separate.

It's the zero which stares so hard
and not because we gravitate to the obvious.

They will miss you in the select committee.

Though volume would be a feeble measure
or the life of someone less real.

We pay because we think we must.

We wait for a tide held up by surface tension.

Fish swim above our landfall.

14 Fixed Photographs

Someone called a period of wandering dreamtime.

These are the photos we save
on which the dead are fixed.

Against a black background.

In this dull city.

The revelations, though, would bring life to any place.
Or sleep, more a narcotic at this level of reversal.

So the voices that seem to originate from objects in a room
hurry here, the way things hurry
toward a background made only of motion.

No detail exempts us. But every detail is a trap.

Please don't imagine anything global.

The carp emerge at feeding time
and look through dangerous film
for the keeper.

These are not the times we waited and planned for.
The carp are often disappointed.

Your face but your location but your phrases.
Do we open the gate to enter
or because we love the feeling of cold metal on our
    hands?

The carp are called koi. We feed them from packets.

You can only hold up one end of history's expectation.
Time goes too slowly, too quickly, disappears.
No detail is forgotten.

We would from a quarter listening
to a new city beholden wake.
Only a debt could spin such gravity
and yet now only names revolve
empty of objects.

There is no postcard to relieve you.

But the ceiling's sagging under the weight
of an archaic snowstorm. The dune eats at the wind
and wakes you tired then cold.

The icicles cannot be tuned as stalactites can.

In one prone photo too saturated with color
too far gone to help now
accuser and salvation switch quarters
atom by atom.

If you give credence to one of the voices.

The madness of a winter of only five days.

If the moment is really all we have.

The adhesions we are helpless to.

As a cup lifts or a starboard signal
but the sounding is faint or vessel uncertain,
your face in the face of a specific nocturne.

You forget the limitations of space.

Distance becomes a kind of future.

Although she wanted more than anything
just to fall asleep.

Someone had said it was merely facing the
blank canvas, or was that a sheet?

Only a beach two thousand miles away would suffice.

Worrying about the idea of place can seem to others
a disconnected activity.

However she turned, wind was never present.
This was testament to a way of addressing the world.

None of the clocks agreed.

Once she had been observed
sleeping beside a log on a beach.

The vehicle stands for the space between places.

She thought her ideas of concealment somehow equaled
    silence.

Her place of clocks and maps.

She particularly wanted to sleep.

If one waits or if one holds back or if one is exuberant or if one insists.

Perhaps anything can or must be said.

The birds would remain
in the afternoon heat
if the breeze picked up
or the air were still.

An echo has three facets.

15 The Way the Room Smells

The precision of any word or the way we use it, here, in the opposite of entry. I.e. pronouns torture us because they're proxies, they're points of contact; for example rumors, spying, breeches of trust. Or here, in the correlative of reason, we may agree on a concept, a production of histories. We find the recent blurry. Nor can grammar aid their procession, the prodigious flight, the diminutive call.

Though they came with intention others said volition.

They keep saying syntax but they mean money.

They pump gas but they could just go home.

Or the streets are washed with fervor.

In this way things are flush.

Their perfume carries in advance.

Her voice was familiar. Its timbre touched a chord.

The dialogues which we might compose
wrinkle too quickly.

Fatigue would sweep them away.
Their core temperatures would rob them.

They would willingly surrender.

Some say succumb.

As in a mood someone mentioned once in temper, in
    pressure
or a skyward superstition which hangs on.

Seasonally or, put another way,
measured by our own need to measure;
we are listening though reported unable.

For sure we have voted to keep the phone from the desk.

Thus sounds emanate or seem to emanate
from objects which ought to be solid.
To say that this causes worry would be overstatement.
But the tides are stronger than usual,
their neaps and springs energetic in a way
that alarms those who believe nature a person.

Perhaps we'd decide to remain away
if the planet were not so remote.

Our objects can't really deceive us.

The mocking bird's list carefully unwinding
like any detail carefully unwound.
It's neither space nor time unwinding.
No details lacking.

It's life can't be severed: these are only photos.

No sheet that loud, no twisted light source,
because if you want to read you will.
In some perfect state of denial or containment.
The sentence unwinds, the story, the animal.

Or those simple dreams
where the dog jumps over the bed
and you remember any act of love.

Here the voice by which we mean a northerly
prevailing by which we picture tundra gusted upon
who ain't a place or was that a different writer
mid-nineteenth century before the two-day warning
or the seven-second delay.

The prevailing voice but the vehicle, unclear and evasive,
is stethoscopic. It's time with or without lists
by whose function we thought perspective would be
    erased.
Just as the infinitive is anticipated – desired? –
or are we closer to a volcanic base by which we picture
basaltic landscapes too young for trees
heat still rising.

They weren't heeding the hour. The prevalent basaltic
    voice
pictured somehow as entwined by which self-sufficiency
springs to mind and concealment.

Here somehow figured. No picture is conjured.
By which place is meant to be released
which could mean voiced or would that be the opposite?
Here no one would expect a reason
which doesn't mean there is one,
through which door a backdrop is seen, windless,
like an anchor pull.

If any record is made, where *is* means
could or might be, the turn they heed
accepting one set of religions,
even their interruptions somehow sacrosanct.

Someone's *this veneer of appearance*
not nearly sufficient, this globe's *over and under*
not nearly sufficient to contain all its errors,
which means whose?

Nor is it the transparency of sound
but rather the expectation that what is ill
can be put right or that any memory
has roots in belief.

Please notice the placement of objects overly finished,
please notice that the way in which they speak
is meant to simulate record.

When the question arises and the hallways fill with light,
where light itself is not a concept,
what is seen in one place may not repeat elsewhere.

Though what is set down is not the same as setting right.
Please notice the conditional state of any penetrant.
The republic is enormous and rests on an alphabet.

The aroma they wished to impose would not linger.
The month had changed yet again.
The subject of heat was not appropriate
but remained on everyone's mind.

The demand was slack.
The dictionary's introduction unreal.
Sorrow is not so overwhelming. But in politics
we settle for the way the room smells.

A color was left as a marker. Some said crimson
others gray. Some called it a note
both missive and musical,
a signature, both mythic and paginated.
Content, she said, but in the sad way.
Or was that wise and sad, a child distracted?

Now any information must be doubted.
The motives are too strong
but the implications seem obvious,
a deck between island and mainland,
gulls in tow but also flying, pictured instead.

They had guessed at his whereabouts. Their concern
was in their own body of knowledge.

The lore is startling.

16 Compounded Capitals

His quill so temporary.
But the sound of it on paper.
Buried in eddies of cloud
the sunlight, the capitals of columns.
Fate's runaway slave. Sleeves too big.

The air is heavy that settles in cuts.

Physically only a visitor, and yet not unpleased.
Furniture set in the center of the room so the periphery
could be paced, without light, at any time or weather.

Shoulders may be put level.
The buried water is warm but dense.

Some claimed any keepsake to be a thing they called an archetype. Yet others divine footsteps from adjoining properties, such as the universal solvency of water, or career hopes dashed to terrazzo floors.

Still others hear someone in a gambling hall, making a killing, pockets full of gemstones, hands full of rough cut.

The phase they call exchange is mistaken for justice, prejudice or the acumen of brokers.
Tables of reference are razed or embellished.

Try the lights and test the plumbing.
Take dimensions and see a future.

Finality is seen slowly sometimes.

Where, if they had come to the crossing of desire and the behavior which causes desire's defeat, a comet had been rumored but not seen. These had been projections, what men in lab coats hire illustrators to portray. The country was younger; the expectations unsullied. She sang Wenceslaus incessantly, the occasion not really of importance. But the rhythms were scary, the argument being something about translation.

Their interjections were always more interesting than their footnotes.

And yet exuberance, in any form, can also catalyze withdrawal.

Somewhere the procession stops, or was that process?

Dreams migrate from the interior, where Clytemnestra prowls in disbelief. Sacrifice and vigilance mar the background they form. A tiny goddess steals to the furthest frontier.

Thus boxed, or rather the ocean, increasing in swell, the very openness they must have read of once, an incarnate idea, or rather any thing as disembodied as space, or re-embodied, localized to the point of arousal, or so we comfort ourselves.

Even the rising fantasy, even the faint legacy of a family vanishing.

We cannot see the lightning but we cannot stop thinking of revenge or at least we think of parity but we cannot see the reason which is how they might explain the language they develop that strives to obscure actions. And it may be a simple shift in barometric pressure, where blood and ink and water spring easily and smoothly, because they know of our attachments to sensation. We have begun to believe that, because their abilities have erased the marks and crosshatchings, anything residual is regressive. Forward, thus, loses its relativity. Or so says their vigilant language.

It was the light before the rain or during the gathering or it was a music from an earlier time tainted in ways we can't know now, or so we compound our interests.

17 The Framed City

Though he had reported once before
on the viscous nature of still water,
there were those who read it differently.
Others had chosen to permanently mark their flesh.
There had been no further steps to decline the novel.

Some found the redundancies intolerable:
not the repeating of subjects but the paths to get there;
not the irreversibility of any action
but the affirmation that the brain is physical so it's all
      physical.

The boys played their gun play still,
yet the obesity of their children never seemed connected.

This was the house of repetition
where everything was incipient.

They dip beneath a sheet of light,
weightless and breathless
doubting the preponderances and spaces
that they themselves contain.

You are steep and steep also means tight.
Then sleep can be sexual.
Thus textures become olfactory.
Efficiency is a crucial factor,
the precepts, marked and annotated,
career, like the sorrow of billiards.

The sentences we inhale
leave only a trace.

But they have given us melodies
to displace thoughts.
We dream of a ship
on its side, careening.

No matter how desperate the words,
the translation appears desperately below,
in matters uncalm.

Perhaps because the nature of any single thing
seems inconstant, memories, for example,
memories or the chain of events
which lead to intervention.

To intervene could also be to counsel caution:
fish usually cannot fly, the plural isn't often singular.
Or physically, as one conversation
may be said to intervene,
from the air, for example,
we come upon a train of thought,
a chain of events,
an incarnadine pattern of speech.

Elusive is the quality of any single thing.

In the barometric world examples are less important.
The schools travel predictably.
A gift is not a gift but a code to be deciphered.
Cement steps replace sand at the shoreline and city
encroaches in narrow streets up to the steps.

A minaret would not surprise us. Its voice, not uncalm,
actually singular.

They dream their home near water, where everything
    counts.
If otherwise noted in other books
the dreamland's hidden, a fortress expository.
Their sweet model posits a climate of change,
a report we now recall.

Their state of grace is less pacific.
Or each state has its own logic.

Theirs is finished in blue tones;
deaf as if alone in a vacant fantasy,
because the music they set in,
each beat, each pad
tipped, dreamed in the lumbar spine.

The picture is framed: the European City.

The other frame is vast beyond pattern.

The first stage was raked because the city's American
and America is steep.

The voice of police pervades any interior.

Assistance is a ticklish thing. Attraction also.

Now tell us of the legend.
The legend is sometimes keyed to a color, sometimes to
texture.

It's hard to see the transactional as subtle,
unless it is scripted.

Lines may also be used. The legend is keyed to smell.
Metal also has an odor.

In Europe they all know each other but walking is
unimpeded. This is one city.

Hills are accounted for. The legend is corporal.
An arch may be useful. We'll opt for paper.

A wall is a wall. The stage is flat. The grid will remain
invisible this time.

Frame and recognition are more texture than taste.

Gold will be used as emphasis.

Even attraction can be complicated.

18 The Room Is Cleaned

The house collapses. Patents from another story
come in. The room is cleaned and emptied.

We're really not the victims of history.

Whose face can we remember from a different dream?
Why does wreckage appear in the subtitles?
Or why can't we speak if we remember so much?

We revolve on the issue of possibly changing.
Those things are late we grasp on history's cusp.

The hour is marked with isotopes
though shoes leave requiems on the story's index.
The angles, always rakish, are always predominant.
This is the ancient singer leaving the water.
His treatise on particles is almost atomic.
From elsewhere comes an anthem, or an ecstasy,
or any barely graspable ephemera.
If this isn't perfection, at least it's redundant.

In your jury's hands
not apocalyptic, not really
in any cherub's eye.

Like water without webbing
insubstantial is the paradise conjoined in judgment.

The use of metaphor is not distasteful,
nor venom, in any small amount.
Who's tupping the white bull now?

For they postulate any angle
believing in occurrence.
They reject the whistles' metals,
the mist urine-diluted
the cherub's renal temper.

You said some power was guiding or hindering you he
    told us
he said, brilliance being in the mind of the analyst.

But then the plot called for smoothness.
A coupling is foreseen. The expectation so painful,
a deadline always sexy.

But my thoughts were literally sucked from the top of
    my head,
she told him you told us he said,
separateness being unique and vacuum a thing unknown.

We are all motives. There is only history and that's the
    painful part,
we said collectively they reported others claimed.

The details of a distant car trip continue to impress
    themselves
in mental images, at inappropriate times.

But can time, they queried, ever truly be inappropriate,
    we remembered she added.

A testy breeze made of electrons. A series of recognitions.

Because absence and variety, in a vague, scene setting sort
    of way,
will render commiseration an invisible shunt.

Form marks us. We tire so quickly now.

19 An Opened Horizon

Over an opened horizon (read: future)
or we remember certain scenes (or believe we do)
which only gets harder, i.e. it spreads out,
a container uncontained, a remnant relished.

We confirm the texture and it is calm.
Our nerves slow at the news. Real storms are forming.
This means political upheaval.
Then how can we speak of weather,
a few drops of rain on the windshield,
the clarity otherwise perfect, we are coding in our steps
     now,
a family gathered, new arrangements, volcanic soil,
one quiet, posted, a record thought, container prepared.

What they call mythology is the summoning of any
     information.

The climate has become unreliable.

They have been known to say things
just for the expedient effect,

though by home they meant any nuclear reaction
i.e. cellular, not military.

The uncertainty of the solar system is of little interest
     now.
This must be adulthood.

By chemical they meant any humor
by which they meant cause.

He dreamed of a dish sufficient to test fate.
Guilt is a process more granular than separate.
She was confused by his meaning of dish.
One will be absent, another included.

Verbs sustain us,
even if the feast solidifies.
Maybe music also.
Order is simulated.

They howled at a planet when opposition occurred.
The jagged flow of lava dried.
We planned an early day.

A hurricane was casually predicted.
And thus the state has servants.

These are colonies, which some don't find alluring.

Or feast days, according to whom,
as siblings do or do not get along
no one can really dominate a phrase
but a darkness sets the foreground for light.
These are the tropics no matter where they are.

Specifically he said my t-shirt is itching me

and they laughed picturing the Polled Herefords of the
    sun god.

That look of disappointment –
silver sheen, bloodless skin.
They had meant to warn us.

20 A Chart Room

They were lucky who read fast.
A forestry of signposts, a dark shade unparalleled.
They chose the period of pieces.
These traits we often ridicule.

But why not ask for that which might be due?

A certain landscape runs through our minds
from a time we would prefer to forget.

The lightning fields were never seen.
The image of a water spout has only been imagined.
The darker the darker the better the better.
We ridicule the use of scale.

Somewhere on a distant piece of land
in a place foreseen or a place evaded
they manage to conjure a chart.

Now they revive with line and legend
something spatial, under a shadow's cover,
fleet, like passing scratches.

Their charted feet, tectonic shoulders;
an arbor rests them, an unknown island.

Someone's music cures them.

If the oasis is a platform, they meant or feared judgment.

An accumulative scale.
Where are the ankles
to inner approbation's feet?

What's manufactured is not always handmade.

Their feet chartered. They recall a numbered statement.
What booms is a name.

Anticipation is practice, a human thing.

Their charted impulse, a foreseen place:
a morning view, warm and volcanic, their feet,
meaning something leads them.

Suddenly a declaration (filter):
the water has warmed, something from far away
has been absorbed.

Or chambered, by which the human hand
is referenced, but once removed, a platform.

By which they mean comfort but the winds are charted.

By the time you hear this an occasion will have arisen.

In a place of purchase.

Or by comfort some manipulation is accepted.

What can anyone else know?

By forest they meant a fern clinging to lava.

They told him this is your temple, manage it.

This summer's lie they abandon,
they who believe that in pronouns lie positioning.

Water floats on water.
We worry that the elements are social.

Because any painting.

Because we hoard sadness.

Picture a room so small
convection is displaced with tightness.

Fog is nearly the icon but acquisition is a stronger idea.
What is certain is an anthem.

Is the physical world a refuge or just a reminder?

Because heat took the word away,
left only an oil slick, colors refracted
in the age when everything's refracted.

We scratched for water and water came out.

In place of purity, temperature grades.

Calls came out.

A hidden geography, imposed, selected.
A signal obscured by fog.

Because by heat we mean air and the world of objects.
It's hard to remember all the names,
because by untouched we mean any clear place or time.
I.e. when the field has been befouled, and by befouled
we mean mentioned in the wrong rhetoric,
and by field we mean a place between places
that could be left alone.

And there are those who pay attention.

We know the clothes they wear
and the way they spell it.
We know how they feel about closure
and pursuing their themes to resolution.

The task's gravity, undeterred by subtleties.

21 Clarity

Her three kisses her trousseau her lids.

Our measurements astride a keep, a kelp bed.

A period an adjustment a reason.

A tension built on a medium we grow to abandon.

The politics they hate to love.

The moment finally arrives.

Night is more than dinner.

On shore on shoal on shore.

Through rock and white caps
or through the sea god's angry triads
nor the hydroplane's conveyance
nor breaking wind (in extremis) before the host.

We have gifts celebrities have borne.
Something shivers our caste.

Earlier we danced without compunction
no mind to the witnessing consul
who slept despite his captain's earthquake.

But stark it was and steep and cool
and the ocean severe it was a place
we got to, returned to.

We end our stories with prepositions.
At our meat we take the tendons.

On the continent they say from the island,
where sex will always be an issue, that caroling interrupts,
by which they mean singing.
But from where does the sound come?

•

No matter how they refute their past
we hear a chorus.
And by chorus we mean something tragic
as if the bystanders didn't have enough violence on their
    minds.

This might be Arizona. An artifact would prove it.
And so the past is slowly stripped away.
These are the landscapes replicated in certain cells.
The imprint can be sung, we imagine.

•

"From the inside of my head I heard commandments."
But these are the body-obsessed eras.

No matter how they refute their sirens,
matter can also refer to mass or masses.
This passage means geography to some,
where maps of transit are stored,

where residues of metals lodge in our brains
and give us directions.

•

Someone said that reason by itself is what? Enough?
Someone seeking resolution was bound to offer that.
History gradually is stripped away.

Possessions remain, artifacts remain, matter
sometimes mass, by which music, ritual, architecture
are all invoked, a ceremony, a placement for chorus.

We mean the politicians or their artifacts or a dust
so fine it flows (viz. some earlier piece)

Credit where credit is doomed.

That there must be contestation.
Or those who believe in their own pleasures.

Heat is released through the controvertible kitchen.

In these days of extreme tides
where fluids become sensate and the moon grows close
we ask in a language received but denatured
the questions once put forward by adversaries.
They only sought to justify themselves.
Or he seemed to pit his guests
rather than seat them.

We forget in our annals the subtle quirks.
Phenomenology is too predictable.

What is intended is abandonment, sometimes called
    divestiture.

Context as a form unto itself?

Then these recurring landscapes may really mean
    something.

They found no way to accommodate his views.
His pleasure was no longer desired.
A pall had fallen over their conversations.

In order not to offend them,
feelings being the most important things,
he tried to remember not to forget
any of his important items.

The epic of description followed him.

And yet it was pleasing: He knew
that he was not bitten.

They were often confused by his clarity.

Times come, he thought.

Los Angeles
1992 – 2002

GREEN INTEGER
Pataphysics and Pedantry

Douglas Messerli, *Publisher*

Essays, Manifestos, Statements, Speeches, Maxims,
Epistles, Diaristic Notes, Narratives, Natural Histories,
Poems, Plays, Performances, Ramblings, Revelations
and all such ephemera as may appear necessary
to bring society into a slight tremolo of confusion
and fright at least.

★

Books in the Green Integer Series

Crowtet I: A Murder of Crows and *The Hyacinth Macaw* Mac Wellman [2000]
Hercules Richelieu and *Nostradamus* Paul Snoek [2000]
Abingdon Square María Irene Fornes [2000]
Sand Dennis Phillips [2002]
Three Masterpieces of Cuban Drama: Plays by Julio Matas,
Carlos Felipe, and *Virgilio Piñera* edited with an Introduction
by Luis F. González-Cruz and Ann Waggoner Aken [2000]
Rectification of Eros Sam Eisenstein [2000]
Drifting Dominic Cheung (Chang Ts'o) [2000]
Gold Fools Gilbert Sorrentino [2001]
Erotic Recipes: A Complete Menu for Male Potency Enhancement Jiao Tong [2000]
The Mysterious Hualien Chen I-chih [2001]

Green Integer EL-E-PHANT Books
[6 x 9 format]

The PIP Anthology of World Poetry of the 20th Century 1
edited with a Preface by Douglas Messerli [2000]
The PIP Anthology of World Poetry of the 20th Century 2
edited with a Preface by Douglas Messerli [2001]
readiness / enough / depends / on Larry Eigner [2000]
Two Fields that Face and Mirror Each Other Martin Nakell [2001]
The School for Atheists: A Novella Arno Schmidt [2001]
Meeting at the Milestone Sigurd Hoel [2002]
Defoe Leslie Scalapino [2002]

BOOKS IN PREPARATION

Islands and Other Essays Jean Grenier
The Doll and *The Doll at Play* Hans Bellmer
[with poetry by Paul Éluard]
American Notes Charles Dickens
Prefaces and Essays on Poetry
William Wordsworth
Confessions of an English Opium-Eater
Thomas De Quincey